INDUSTRY JOBS

JOBS IN AGRICULTURE

BY CYNTHIA KENNEDY HENZEL

Core Library

An Imprint of Abdo Publishing
abdobooks.com

Cover image: Poultry farm workers feed birds, keep enclosures clean, and gather eggs.

abdobooks.com

Published by Abdo Publishing, a division of ABDO, PO Box 398166, Minneapolis, Minnesota 55439.

Printed in the United States of America, North Mankato, Minnesota.
052023
092023

THIS BOOK CONTAINS RECYCLED MATERIALS

Cover Photo: Janie Airey/Getty Images
Interior Photos: Bestami Bodruk/Anadolu Agency/Getty Images, 4–5; Mustafa Hassona/Anadolu Agency/Getty Images, 6; Kilito Chan/Getty Images, 10; Frederic J. Brown/AFP/Getty Images, 12–13, 42 (middle); Jean-Pierre Clatot/AFP/Getty Images, 14; Michael Conroy/AP Images, 17; iStockphoto, 20–21, 43 (middle top); Shutterstock Images, 22 (corn, soybeans), 30 (top middle, top right, bottom middle), 43 (middle bottom); Edwin Remsburg/VW Pics/Getty Images, 24; Robert F. Bukaty/AP Images, 26, 45; GC Shutter/Getty Images, 28–29, 43 (bottom); Hennadii H/Shutterstock Images, 30 (top left, bottom right); Amanita Silvicora/Shutterstock Images, 30 (bottom left); Zhang Bowen/Xinhua News Agency/Getty Images, 34–35, 43 (middle); Michael Holahan/The Augusta Chronicle/AP Images, 38; Amanda Caroline da Silva/Getty Images, 40; Budimir Jevtic/Shutterstock Images, 42 (top); Carmen Jaspersen/Picture Alliance/Getty Images, 42 (middle top); Sandy Huffaker/Stringer/Getty Images, 42 (middle bottom); Alan Campbell/Rocky Mount Telegram/AP Images, 42 (bottom); Hector Rio/AFP/Getty Images, 43 (top)

Editor: Laura Stickney
Series Designer: Katharine Hale

Library of Congress Control Number: 2022949106

Publisher's Cataloging-in-Publication Data

Names: Henzel, Cynthia Kennedy, author.
Title: Jobs in agriculture / by Cynthia Kennedy Henzel
Description: Minneapolis, Minnesota: Abdo Publishing Company, 2024 | Series: Industry jobs | Includes online resources and index.
Identifiers: ISBN 9781098290863 (lib. bdg.) | ISBN 9781098277048 (ebook)
Subjects: LCSH: Occupations--Juvenile literature. | Farming--Biography--Juvenile literature. | Agriculture--Biography--Juvenile literature. | Farming--Juvenile literature.
Classification: DDC 630.203--dc23

CONTENTS

CHAPTER ONE

A DAY IN THE LIFE OF A BEEKEEPER

Raul yawned as he put on his bee suit. He wasn't a morning person, but it was best to check the hives when it was cool outside. The bee suit was thick, white cotton coveralls that protected him from stings. The light color kept bees calmer. Raul added a hat with a wide brim and a veil of netting to protect his face. He made sure there were no gaps around his neck. Then he put on long gloves.

Beekeepers collect honey from beehives to be sold at markets. They're also responsible for making sure beehives stay healthy and clean.

Beekeepers are also called apiary workers. They must be able to handle beehives carefully and calmly.

Raul's partner, Virginia, was already at the hive. She was lighting the smoke pot. The smoke pot created thick black smoke to keep the bees away from the beekeepers. Virginia lit a handful of dried pine needles and put them in the pot. She gave the pot a puff of air to get it blazing. Then she added more fuel on the top and closed the lid.

CHECKING THE HIVE

Raul cracked the lid of the first hive, and Virginia puffed smoke into the box. The bees moved away from the smoke. Raul removed the lid of the hive, and Virginia puffed smoke between the wooden frames. The frames held sheets of beeswax or plastic imprinted with hexagon-shaped cells. These were where bees stored honey and the queen bee laid eggs.

Raul used a flat tool to pull out some of the frames. He looked at them carefully. He saw no evidence of

PERSPECTIVES

HONEYBEES AND NATIVE BEES

Honeybees originally came from Europe. They were brought to North America to provide honey. Today, many farmers rent honeybees to pollinate crops. Approximately 1 billion honeybees live in North America. Beekeepers worry about keeping colonies alive, but few people worry about the continent's native bees. Native bees are disappearing because they can't compete with honeybees for food. "Beekeeping is for people; it's not a conservation practice," says conservation biologist Sheila Colla.

CAPTURING A WILD HIVE

People sometimes find a swarm of bees in trees near their homes. They call beekeepers to remove the bees. A beekeeper captures the bees by putting a box or bucket under the swarming bees. Then they shake the branch. The clump of bees falls into the container. If the queen is with them, the bees settle down. If not, they fly out, and the beekeeper must try again. Once the swarm is in the container with the queen, the beekeeper takes the bees home to start a new hive.

disease or dangerous mites that could cause the bees in the hive to die. He checked for eggs in the cells. Yes! The queen was laying eggs. Virginia recorded the date, time, and what Raul found.

Raul replaced the bag of sugar water that gave the bees extra food. Bees normally eat honey, but this hive would soon travel from South Dakota to California to pollinate almonds. They needed extra food for the trip. The bee farm rented hives to farmers who needed pollinators for their crops. There were too few native pollinators to pollinate the huge almond groves when they bloomed. Altogether, US almond producers needed 2.5 million hives in 2020 to pollinate their crops when the trees bloomed. Renting out hives provided a lot of income to the bee farm.

Raul reassembled the square boxes of the hive. The bees buzzed angrily and crawled over him. The bee suit protected him, but he was still a little nervous. The team moved on to check the next hive.

After morning inspections, the beekeepers took off their bee suits. They went to the equipment shed to repair some older hives. A beekeeper never knew when someone might call about a swarm of bees.

THE AGRICULTURE INDUSTRY

Beekeeping is just one job in the agriculture industry. Some farm workers breed and care for animals. Other farm workers plant, tend, harvest, and process crops, such as wheat or strawberries. However, less than 2 percent of agricultural work is done on a farm or ranch.

Other agricultural workers invent new ways to use water and land more efficiently. They come up with ways to dispose of farm waste safely. Some jobs are done in laboratories. Researchers develop new seeds and methods to make food production more efficient. One in 12 Americans works in a job related to agriculture. Agricultural jobs, from picking apples to inventing robot harvesters, are essential to feed the world.

FURTHER EVIDENCE

Chapter One talks about the importance of bees for pollination. Explore the website below to find out more about honeybees and how they are connected to people. Find a quote from the website to show the importance of honeybees. Does the quote support the information in the chapter or add to the existing information?

HONEYBEE FIELD GUIDE

abdocorelibrary.com/jobs-in-agriculture

Many jobs in the agriculture industry involve working with plants and animals.

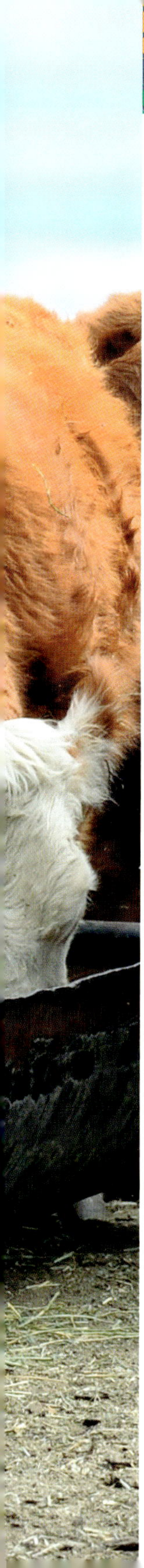

CHAPTER TWO

RAISING ANIMALS

One of the largest agricultural industries is supplying meat for food. Ranchers raise animals for meat and other products, such as wool and leather. Cattle ranches have ranch hands who watch over livestock, which are farm animals such as cattle and sheep. These animals roam hundreds of acres of land. During the winter, ranch hands provide feed for livestock. They might also manage the health of animals, giving them treatments to prevent diseases or parasites.

Ranch hands must be comfortable working around large animals and unafraid to get their hands dirty.

Many dairy workers use automatic or robotic milking machines to milk cows.

Ranch hands generally ride horses or all-terrain vehicles (ATVs). They must be strong and willing to work long hours. Ranch hands must work whenever there is a need to get something done. It is useful to know how to fix things, from fences to tractors. Most ranch hands learn their skills on the job.

The main responsibility of dairy workers is to milk cows several times a day. Cows must be moved into a milking barn. Strict regulations require that facilities, milking equipment, and milk storage containers be clean. Cows must be fed and checked for any illnesses. Workers also care for young calves. These skills are often learned at entry-level positions. Dairy managers have higher level positions that may require a college degree. They are responsible for keeping detailed records about each cow. They also oversee pastures, equipment, and workers.

CHEESE GRADERS

A specialty agricultural job is making cheese. Cheese taste testers, or graders, must identify the quality of more than 100 types of cheese. Most learn the skill working as cheesemakers. Official cheese graders need a license. They must pass an exam to identify the quality of the look, taste, texture, and smell of 12 different cheeses. They must then smell ten different mixtures and identify the unique aroma from each one that is found in cheese.

Once animals go to market, meat packers are responsible for preparing the meat for restaurants and homes. They make sure the meat is not spoiled. Then they cut the meat into pieces using knives or large machines. Some meat packers grind meat into hamburger or make sausage. Meat is then packaged and labeled. Meat packer jobs require a high school diploma. It is useful to have experience in handling sharp tools. Meat packers must also follow government rules about handling meat. These rules help make sure the meat is safe to eat.

Poultry farms raise chickens for meat or eggs. On farms that sell eggs, workers feed chickens and make sure they have clean water and barns. New chicks need special attention to make sure they stay warm. When hens lay eggs, workers gather them. The eggs then move to a processing area where they are washed and candled. Candling means passing the egg in front of a bright light to check whether the inside of the egg is good. Eggs are sorted by size. They are then packaged and shipped to stores. Working on a poultry farm requires a high school diploma or associate degree.

AQUACULTURE AND INSECT FARMS

One growing industry is aquaculture, or raising food in water instead of on land. Fish such as salmon or tilapia

Some fish farmers set up floating tanks or enclosures offshore, while others set up specially designed tanks on land.

are raised in enclosed artificial tanks. Some jobs on fish farms require a high school diploma. Higher-level jobs require workers to monitor water quality. They keep chemicals in the water in balance and watch for signs of disease. This helps fish stay healthy. These jobs require a bachelor's degree in biology or management.

Aquaculture managers supervise other farm workers and keep track of money. They are in charge of selling and transporting the fish. Researchers in aquaculture require a graduate degree. They study the best ways to design farms and keep fish healthy.

Another growing industry is insect farming. Insects provide protein and vitamins at a lower cost than traditional food animals. Insects also take up less land to grow and are better for the environment.

Crickets and mealworms are used in food for fish, chickens, and even humans. Insects are raised indoors in plastic and cardboard boxes. Workers feed insects and maintain temperature and humidity. Then they collect the insects and freeze them for sale. Most workers are trained on the job.

PERSPECTIVES

ETHICS AND INSECTS

People don't know much about insects' lives. Researchers know that insects communicate. They learn from past experiences. Honeybees understand numbers and the concept of zero. On insect farms, insects are kept in crowded boxes. They are killed by freezing or shredding. People don't know if they feel stress or pain. Some people concerned with animal welfare oppose farming insects this way. They think insects are not being treated humanely and that more research is needed to understand what humane insect treatment looks like.

STRAIGHT TO THE SOURCE

Cowboys herded cattle across the prairie. These workers faced many hardships. Teddy Blue Abbot, a cowboy who worked in the 1800s, wrote about his experience:

> *I believe the worst hardship we had on the trail was loss of sleep. There was never enough sleep. Our day wouldn't end till about nine o'clock, when we grazed the herd onto the bed ground. And after that every man in the [group] except the boss and horse wrangler and cook would have to stand two hours' night guard. . . . [After night guard I slept] till the cook yelled, "Roll out," at half past three. So I would get maybe five hours' sleep when the weather was nice and everything smooth and pretty. . . . If it wasn't so nice, you'd be lucky to sleep an hour. But the wagon rolled on in the morning just the same.*

Source: Cody Assmann. "Cowboy Life in the 1800s: Primary Sources." *Frontier Life*, 23 Dec. 2020, frontierlife.net. Accessed 16 Aug. 2022.

BACK IT UP

The author is using evidence to support a point. Write a paragraph describing his point. Identify two or three pieces of evidence he uses to make his point.

SIDEHILL 9550

CHAPTER THREE

GROWING CROPS

While some agricultural jobs focus on livestock, others focus on plants. Crops include grains such as corn or wheat. They also include fruits and vegetables. Farmers grow crops used to make food for people, as well as for pets and farm animals. Other farmers supply cotton for cloth or lumber for construction and paper.

Small family farms depend on the labor of the farmer and his or her family. These farms may also hire extra help at times.

Most of the corn grown in the United States comes from farms in the Corn Belt, a region stretching from Indiana to Nebraska.

MAJOR FOOD CROPS GROWN IN THE UNITED STATES

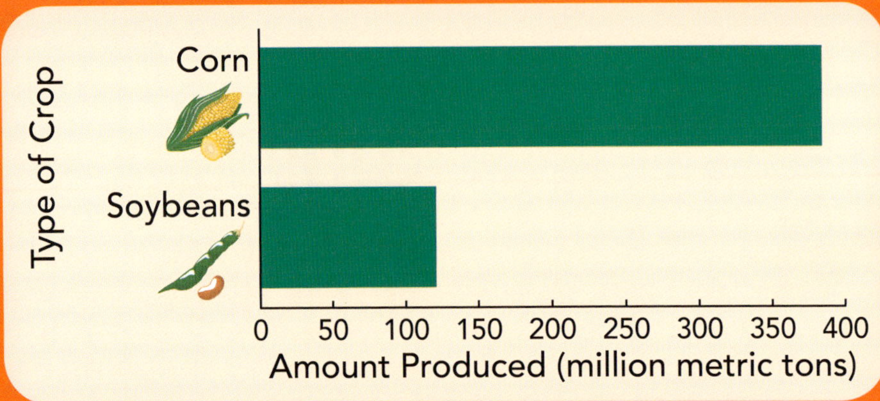

There are many different food crops grown in the United States. In 2021–2022, the top crops were corn and soybeans. Why do you think these are the major crops in the country? Why might farmers choose to grow corn and soybeans instead of another crop?

Ongoing education is important. Changes in technology and new research into better farming practices can make farms more profitable.

Industrial farms may cover thousands of acres. Agricultural managers run these large businesses. This job requires good organizational and communication skills. Agricultural managers are responsible for hiring and supervising workers.

They buy and maintain equipment. They are also in charge of budgeting. This job often requires some college education.

Most farms depend on heavy equipment to plow fields, plant seeds, fertilize soil, and harvest crops. Tractors, harvesters, and other equipment need trained operators. Operators need to know how the machines work. They need to be careful and follow instructions. They often learn these skills through vocational training or on the job.

FUNGUS FARMS

Many types of fungi are farmed for their mushrooms. Mushrooms are the fruiting part of the fungi. Workers on mushroom farms usually work indoors. Mushrooms require specific temperatures and humidity at different stages of growth. Workers must carefully check the material in which the mushrooms are growing. They make sure the material isn't contaminated by harmful mold or bacteria.

Growing vegetables and fruits requires a lot of hard manual labor. It is backbreaking work to pick thousands

Agricultural equipment operators use machines such as combines, threshers, and tractors to harvest crops.

of vegetables or fruits. Workers are sometimes paid by how much they pick, so they must be efficient to earn good wages. Many of these jobs require migrant workers. Migrant workers move from farm to farm as seasons change. The United States has a severe shortage of farm workers. Few young people want to do this difficult work for low wages.

AQUACULTURE CROPS

One popular aquaculture crop is seaweed. As a result, there is a rising demand for workers. Farmers grow seaweed that is used in sushi, sauces, and many other food products. Farmers grow seaweed on longlines placed 4 to 8 feet (1.2–2.4 m) below the water's surface. The long blades, or leaves, are harvested in spring.

Seaweed is a fairly new crop. The National

PERSPECTIVES

DANGEROUS JOBS

Araceli Ruiz arrived in California from Mexico when she was 19 years old. She worked in fields picking vegetables to earn money for her children. Sometimes she worked where pesticides had been sprayed. She even worked when pregnant with her son, who later developed health problems because of his mother's pesticide exposure. Today, Ruiz works to warn other women about farm chemicals. "We're here and doing all this work, but we are not given the path to . . . raise our families without the fear of it one day being ripped apart," Ruiz says. "It would definitely be appreciated if our government. . . saw us as essential."

In the United States, many people have started seaweed farms off the shores of New England, the Pacific Northwest, and Alaska.

Oceanic and Atmospheric Administration (NOAA) is researching the best way to grow the industry. The industry needs people who want to participate in the increasing number of small seaweed farms. NOAA provides training to people who want to grow seaweed. The industry also needs researchers such as biologists to study plants. Chemists study the best water conditions for growing seaweed.

Algae are also promising aquaculture crops. They can be used for food, animal feed, and biofuel. Algae grow in harsh environments, so they do not compete with other crops for high-quality soil or water. Biologists, chemists, and conservationists study how algae farming could help produce enough food and energy for Earth's rising population. This new field needs people with agriculture degrees who can develop the best means of growing algae. Chefs are needed to invent new ways to use algae in foods. Chemists are needed to figure out how to use algae in processed food to improve nutrition.

EXPLORE ONLINE

Chapter Three talks about industrial farms. The article at the website below goes into more depth on this topic. Does the article answer any of the questions you had about industrial farms?

10 THINGS YOU SHOULD KNOW ABOUT INDUSTRIAL FARMING

abdocorelibrary.com/jobs-in-agriculture

CHAPTER FOUR

FOOD MANUFACTURING AND TECHNOLOGY

In 2020, 2.6 million agricultural workers worked on US farms. Another 2 million worked in food manufacturing. Food manufacturing involves making farm products ready to send to homes or restaurants. Almost 30 percent of these jobs are in meat processing. Another 15 percent are in bakeries, followed by 12 percent in the beverage industry.

Manufacturing includes jobs such as packaging, canning, or freezing fruits

Production facility managers oversee day-to-day operations, such as worker safety training, machine repair, and cleaning.

PRODUCING BREAD

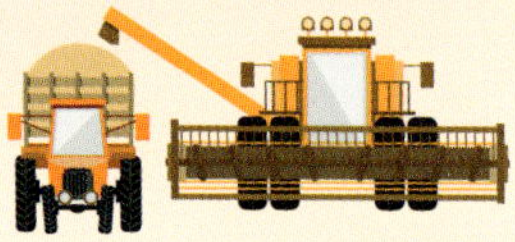

Wheat is harvested at a farm.

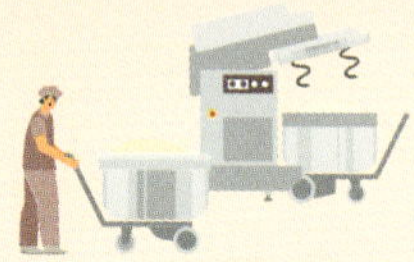

Wheat is processed into bread and wheat products at a processing facility.

The bread is transported to warehouses.

The bread is stored at warehouses.

The bread is transported to stores to be sold.

Bread is on your dinner table.

It takes many kinds of workers to make the bread people eat. Wheat needs to be harvested, processed, and transported to stores. Why do you think it's important for wheat to go through these steps? What would happen if there weren't workers to harvest, process, or transport it?

and vegetables. Other manufacturers process milk products, mill flour from wheat, or produce oil from seeds. Many of these careers have on-the-job training. Workers must operate machinery quickly and carefully. Production facility managers require more training or college degrees. They make sure workers are safe and machinery is maintained properly.

The US government inspects agricultural products for safety. Generally, agricultural inspectors work for government agencies such as the United States Department of Agriculture (USDA). They visit workplaces to inspect products and make sure businesses are following safety regulations.

Some entry-level positions in food inspection require a high school diploma. But most agricultural inspectors need an associate degree or higher degrees in biology, animal science, or agricultural science. Inspectors are required to keep up with new government regulations for producing and processing food.

TECHNOLOGY

As farm sizes increase, agriculture becomes more dependent on specialized machines. Agricultural mechanics maintain and repair machinery. This includes giant harvesters and machines that sort fruits into different sizes. Because specialized machines are often

AG PILOTS

Ag pilots, once known as crop dusters, are pilots who fly over fields spraying chemicals or releasing seed. This job is changing. Today, young pilots train in new technology and techniques for applying chemicals that are safer for the environment. Planes have GPS devices that guide pilots so they only spray where needed. They use an electronic mapping system to apply chemicals in the best amounts. Ag pilots are in demand. Many people begin by mixing chemicals and loading or fixing planes. Then they train to get a special pilot's license.

complex, this work requires an education in mechanics. Huge farm machines require servicing to check that they are ready to be used. Farmers cannot afford to have broken harvesters at harvest time. They only have a small window of time before crops go bad or are damaged by severe weather.

Other jobs involve technology such as robots. Tractors now do much of the planting, spraying, and harvesting. But researchers are developing robots to make these jobs more efficient. GPS specialists use drones to view large areas.

These drones can detect signs of problems. Finding problems early helps farmers save money. These jobs often require college or technical training.

Irrigating, or watering crops, is also necessary on many farms. Farmers need people to design irrigation systems. They also need people to install and maintain those systems. These jobs require technical training and on-the-job experience.

PERSPECTIVES

THE MEGADROUGHT

Each year, less water is available in the West. In Utah, farming uses about 75 percent of the state's water. Most of the water is used to grow hay for animal feed. People in the state use about 12 percent of the water for their homes. People in cities are asked to conserve water by not watering outside plants. Many city people feel that farmers are getting too much water. Farming is only 2 percent of the economy, but lack of water keeps other industries from growing. Governments permit some farmers to use less water, but many farmers do not feel this is necessary. They believe better technology will mean less waste and enough water for everyone.

CHAPTER FIVE

SCIENCE AND EDUCATION

Many agricultural jobs are done in a laboratory or classroom. These agricultural workers need a college degree. Chemists develop new types of fertilizers and pesticides. Soil scientists investigate how soils can hold in nutrients and water.

Geneticists study the genes of seeds. They make changes in the genes so that crops are more resistant to pests, need less water, or grow faster. These new seeds are

Soil scientists collect soil samples and do experiments to figure out what types of soil are best for growing different plants.

often planted on industrial farms, which increases production. Other scientists work with animal cells to grow artificial meat in laboratories. Growing a steak from cells in a lab would mean people wouldn't have to worry about animals being treated inhumanely. These jobs often require advanced degrees in biology, animal science, or genetics.

Land management specialists are conservationists who

PERSPECTIVES

MONOCULTURE

Monoculture is farming by growing only one type of crop in a field. Many people use monoculture because it increases production. It takes less effort, knowledge, and technology to grow one crop instead of many crops. More production means more money. Industrial farms often use monoculture to increase profits. But others oppose monoculture because it can be bad for the environment. They point out that pests and disease are more common on fields with only one crop. This means more pesticides are used. Monoculture also upsets the soil balance by overusing certain nutrients or bacteria. This makes soil less fertile and increases erosion. Poor soil means more fertilizer is used.

help ranchers and farmers use their land sustainably. Land management specialists go to college. They study the best ways to use fertilizers, pesticides, and water. They learn about how to graze pastures without damaging grass or causing erosion. They research new methods of plowing, plant spacing, or growing cover crops. Cover crops are not used for food. Instead, they are grown to protect the soil from washing away with rain or blowing away with wind.

Agricultural engineers design new machines and processes for agricultural production. Some machines make workers more productive by making their work easier. This way, they don't get so tired. Engineers also design new irrigation systems that waste less water. These jobs often require a college education.

TEACHING AND COMMUNICATION

Jobs that communicate research and best practices to farmers and ranchers are important. Every state has colleges with extension services. These agencies

Some farmers work with agricultural camps and organizations for kids, such as 4-H.

hire people who are knowledgeable about agriculture in their regions. They communicate with farmers and ranchers to help them grow better crops and manage their land.

Universities hire professors to educate the next generation in agricultural sciences. The field is constantly changing. Agriculture is seriously affected by climate change and greenhouse gases. To grow the world's food, students must learn to adapt to new technology, crops, and methods. Some people are studying how new agricultural practices could support carbon sinks. These are places that take in more carbon dioxide than they release.

Getting started in farming is difficult. Some family farms are passed on to children, but lots of agricultural land is purchased by industrial farms. For new farmers, it's difficult to borrow money to buy land and farming equipment. The United States wants to encourage

FFA AND 4-H

The National Future Farmers of America (FFA) Organization is a program in local schools. FFA classes teach basic agricultural skills such as caring for animals. The organization also helps students gain leadership roles in their community and at a national level. It offers scholarships to students interested in pursuing agricultural jobs in college. Another national organization is 4-H. It provides after-school programs for young people to learn about agriculture. 4-H encourages students to explore their interests through projects, such as raising livestock and gardening.

Agriculture professors often specialize in one area, such as soil science or food science. They use their expertise to teach college students.

more young people to become farmers. Under the Inflation Reduction Act, the USDA is granting money to struggling farmers. It also provides money to states, American Indian tribes, and Historically Black Colleges and Universities to encourage diversity in agricultural jobs.

Agriculture is an important field that needs workers at all levels of education. Because of new technology and climate change, it can be challenging work. But there is something for everyone who wants to work in agriculture, from working with animals to doing cutting-edge research in a laboratory.

STRAIGHT TO THE
SOURCE

Candace Laing is the vice president of Nutrien, a supplier of farm products and services. She says the challenge of industrial farming is feeding the world while protecting the planet:

> *Agriculture is one of the most exciting sectors now because the world has never needed more out of this sector. And that is because agriculture can bring climate solutions. As much as the sector generates [greenhouse gases], we have an exciting path forward to [use] our soils with natural carbon sinks. . . . The world is really excited about what agriculture can deliver in terms of protecting both people and the planet.*

Source: Georgie Smith. "Agriculture Is Having a Moment: The Next Ag Evolution Is Here." *US Farmers and Ranchers in Action*, 1 June 2021, usfarmersandranchers.org. Accessed 22 Sept. 2022.

CHANGING MINDS

This text passage argues that farmers are also conservationists. Imagine you have a friend who does not agree. Write a short essay to convince them this is true.

JOB LIST

Agricultural engineers design new machines or processes that make agriculture more efficient.

Agricultural inspectors visit food processing facilities to make sure businesses are following regulations to keep food safe.

Ranchers are responsible for the daily care of cattle on a ranch. This includes feeding, health care, and taking the cattle to market.

Migrant farm workers move from farm to farm picking fruits and vegetables as seasons change and new crops ripen.

Extension agents visit farms to help farmers use the best techniques and products to increase quality and production. They may also work with agricultural programs for kids.

Geneticists study genes. They may change genes in seeds to create new varieties of plants that are more resistant to disease, use less water, or produce more food.

Mechanics maintain and repair farm machinery.

Soil scientists research how soil can be made more productive and how to protect soil from erosion.

Meat packers check the quality of meat and prepare different cuts of meat using knives or industrial machinery.

Production facility managers organize work processes and oversee workers to make sure food gets to retailers quickly.

STOP AND THINK

Another View

In Chapter Five, the author of this book discusses changing the genes of seeds and growing meat from cells in a lab. As you know, every source is different. Ask a librarian or another adult to help you find a second source about one of these subjects. Write a short essay comparing and contrasting the new source's point of view with that of this book's author. What is the point of view of each author? How are they similar and why? How are they different and why?

Take a Stand

This book talks about many different jobs in the agricultural industry. Which job do you think sounds the most interesting? Why?

You Are There

Imagine you have a new job working with bees. Write a short story about how you prepare for work and how you feel on your first day caring for bees. What do you like or dislike about your new job?

Dig Deeper

After reading this book, what questions do you still have about aquaculture? With an adult's help, find a few reliable sources that can help you answer your questions. Write a paragraph about what you learn.

GLOSSARY

biofuel
fuel made from things that were recently living, such as algae or corn

conservationist
a person who acts to protect and restore the natural environment

erosion
the loss of soil caused by water washing it away or wind blowing it away

genes
the basic units in the body that pass characteristics from parents to children

greenhouse gas
a gas that traps heat in Earth's atmosphere

pesticides
chemicals used to kill insects that harm plants and crops

pollinate
to move pollen from one flower to another so the plant will produce seeds or fruit

sustainable
able to be kept at the same level

swarm
a large number of bees moving together to a new location

vocational training
classes that teach skills in a particular craft or type of work

ONLINE RESOURCES

To learn more about jobs in agriculture, visit our free resource websites below.

Core Library CONNECTION
FREE! COMMON CORE MULTIMEDIA RESOURCES

Visit **abdocorelibrary.com** or scan this QR code for free Common Core resources for teachers and students, including vetted activities, multimedia, and booklinks, for deeper subject comprehension.

Booklinks NONFICTION NETWORK
FREE! ONLINE NONFICTION RESOURCES

Visit **abdobooklinks.com** or scan this QR code for free additional online weblinks for further learning. These links are routinely monitored and updated to provide the most current information available.

LEARN MORE

Castaldo, Nancy. *The Farm That Feeds Us*. Words & Pictures, 2020.

Kerr, Elissa. *Honey Harvest*. Scenic Route, 2022.

O'Brien, Cynthia. *The Impact of Food and Farming*. Crabtree, 2020.

INDEX

About the Author

Cynthia Kennedy Henzel has a BS in social studies education and an MS in geography. She has worked as a teacher in many countries. Currently, she writes fiction and nonfiction books and develops education materials for social studies, history, science, and ELL students. She has written more than 100 books and 150 stories for young people.